MW01116378

WRITING FOR SOCIAL JUSTICE

JOURNAL AND WORKBOOK

MAGGIE SOKOLIK

WAYZGOOSE PRESS

Copyright © 2019 by Wayzgoose Press

All rights reserved.

No part of this book may be reproduced in any form or by any electronic or mechanical means, including information storage and retrieval systems, without written permission from the author, except for the use of brief quotations in a book review.

Cover design by DJ Rogers for Bookbranders.

Editing by Dorothy Zemach.

CONTENTS

WRITING FOR SOCIAL JUSTICE

LOGOS, ETHOS, PATHOS

JOURNAL

WRITING FOR SOCIAL JUSTICE

WHAT IS SOCIAL JUSTICE?

Look around on the internet or different print publications and you will find a lot of definitions of social justice. The important thing is that you define it for yourself.

For example, here's a partial definition from Wikipedia:

> Social justice is a concept of fair and just relations between the individual and society. This is measured by the explicit and tacit terms for the distribution of wealth, opportunities for personal activity, and social privileges. In Western as well as in older Asian cultures, the concept of social justice has often referred to the process of ensuring that individuals fulfill their societal roles and receive what was their due from society. In the current global grassroots movements for social justice, the emphasis has been on the breaking of barriers for social mobility, the creation of safety nets and economic justice.

Find and read at least three definitions of social justice. After you've read three definitions, write out your own definition of social justice here.

_____

FOUR SPHERES OF SOCIAL JUSTICE WRITING

Writing for social justice can be divided into four areas:

- Personal writing
- Writing to affect your community
- Writing to affect nations
- Writing to change the world

Different types of documents are often associated with each of these types of writing, but there is a considerable amount of overlap.

Personal Writing

In the sphere of writing for social justice, personal writing often involves journals and diaries, blog posts, social media posts, and any other writing that is intended to express oneself, often just for self-edification.

Writing to Affect Your Community

Typical documents might include letters or emails to local officials, petitions about local issues, newsletter or local newspaper opinion pieces, flyers and posters, and so on.

Writing to Affect Nations

This writing can include all of the things mentioned in the previous paragraph, but might also take on published works such as writing opinion pieces for national publications, articles for magazines, or any other writing with a larger scope in mind.

Writing to Change the World

As lofty as this sounds, we have lots of examples of writing to change the world. Published essayists and writers of nonfiction and fiction are associated with this genre. Of course, podcasts, radio shows, pieces of journalism, and published satire also fall in this category.

The question for you is, what are your aspirations? Do you want to explore your own mind to discover what matters most to you? Then, personal writing may satisfy you. Or, do you want to shake up the political system and find justice for others?

Take a moment to write out what your writing aspirations are.

Question: What type of writing will help you change your world? Explain your answer.

_____

_____

_____

_____

_____

THE ISSUES

What are the issues that matter to you? Take some time to list them here. If you aren't sure, use the journal in the second half of this book to help you explore more ideas through writing.

Personal

List ten things that you could improve in your own life to create a more just society. (For example, learn to be more tolerant of those different from you; practice charity, etc.)

1. _____
2. _____
3. _____
4. _____
5. _____
6. _____
7. _____
8. _____
9. _____
10. _____

Local

List ten problems that you feel need to be addressed in your local community.

1. _____
2. _____
3. _____
4. _____
5. _____
6. _____
7. _____
8. _____
9. _____
10. _____

National

List ten issues that you feel need to be changed in your country.

1. _____
2. _____
3. _____
4. _____
5. _____
6. _____
7. _____
8. _____
9. _____
10. _____

Global

List ten issues that you feel need to be addressed on a global scale.

1. _____

2. _____
3. _____
4. _____
5. _____
6. _____
7. _____
8. _____
9. _____
10. _____

AREAS OF INTEREST

In addition to the four spheres of social justice writing, there are also a near countless number of areas of interest. Some potential areas that intersect with social justice are listed here. Next to each one, write a bit about what you know about that area, or what concerns you. Then, add ten more areas.

1. Religion _____
   _____
   _____
   _____

2. Poverty _____
   _____
   _____
   _____

3. Disabilities _____
   _____
   _____
   _____

4. Race/ethnicity _____
   _____

5. Human trafficking _____

_____

6. _____

_____

7. _____

_____

8. _____

_____

9. _____

_____

10. _____

_____

11. _____

_____

12. _____

_____

13. _____

_____

14. _____

_____

_____

15. _____

_____

_____

LOGOS, ETHOS, PATHOS

RHETORIC AND ITS USES

When writing to change a situation, you are writing to persuade an audience, even if that audience is just you.

In classical rhetoric, there are three modes of persuasion, called *logos, ethos,* and *pathos.*

Logos

Logos, as should be apparent from its name, is an appeal to *logic.* Examples of *logos* include using facts, statistics, examples from texts, and citing credible authorities on a subject. *Logos* is the Greek word for "word," but the full definition goes beyond that, and can be fully defined as "the word or that by which the inward thought is expressed" and, "the inward thought itself"[1]. The word "logic" comes from *logos.*

Ethos

Ethos is an ethical appeal. An ethical appeal tries to persuade an audience by showing that the writer is a person of credibility and good character. Writers develop *ethos* by choosing appropriate vocabulary for both the topic and the audience. It is also developed by writing in a way that seems unbiased, demonstrates your expertise, and uses correct grammar.

Pathos

Pathos is an emotional appeal. When you use *pathos* in writing, you are trying to get your audience to feel a particular emotion: sympathy, anger, pity, etc.

Sophisticated writers might employ more than one of these types of appeals when trying to persuade an audience of an idea.

---

1. http://www.perseus.tufts.edu/hopper/text?doc=Perseus:text:1999.04.0058: entry%3Dlo/gos

LETTER FROM BIRMINGHAM JAIL

"The Letter from Birmingham Jail" is an open letter written on April 16, 1963, by Martin Luther King, Jr., defending the idea of nonviolent resistance to racism. He claims in the letter that people have a moral responsibility to break unjust laws. He recommends taking direct action rather than waiting for justice to come through legislative and judicial channels. Responding to being referred to as an "outsider," King writes, "Injustice anywhere is a threat to justice everywhere."

The letter is currently under copyright in the USA, so it cannot be printed in this book. However, you can find it in multiple places online and in print.

Find a copy of the letter. Print it out if you can and write notes on it. Identify areas where Dr. King uses *pathos*, *logos*, and *ethos*.

Here's the first paragraph, with my comments — yours may differ.

> While confined here in the Birmingham city jail[1], I came across your recent statement calling our present activities "unwise and untimely." Seldom, if ever, do I pause to answer criticism of my work and ideas. If I sought to answer all of the criticisms that cross my desk, my secretaries would be engaged in little else in the course of the day, and I

would have no time for constructive work.[2] But since I feel that you are men of genuine good will[3] and your criticisms are sincerely set forth, I would like to answer your statement in what I hope will be patient and reasonable terms.[4]

---

1. This phrase uses pathos; King appeals to the reader's sympathy with his being in jail.
2. The preceding sentence appeals to logic. He is stating the facts of his situation.
3. This is an appeal to ethos, or authority.
4. Another appeal to logic, or logos.

FIND EXAMPLES

Now that you have a sense of how these rhetorical devices are used, find four more examples. You can look online, in magazine articles, in advertising—wherever you normally read. Write about what you found, and what appeals they use.

Example 1

Type of document: _____

Use of rhetorical devices: _____

_____

_____

_____

_____

_____

Example 2

Type of document: _____

Use of rhetorical devices: _____

_____

_____

_____

_____

_____

Example 3

Type of document: _____

Use of rhetorical devices: _____

_____

_____

_____

_____

_____

Example 4

Type of document: _____

Use of rhetorical devices: _____

_____

_____

_____

LOGICAL FALLACIES

Logical fallacies are errors in logic, typically made by misusing persuasive tactics. There are dozens of such fallacies, but I'll list ten of the most important ones.

Some of these fallacies retain their original Latin names, although most are known in English by more common names.

1. *Ad Hominem*
2. Straw Man
3. Appeal to Ignorance
4. False Dilemma
5. Slippery Slope
6. Circular Reasoning
7. Overgeneralization
8. Red Herring
9. *Tu Quoque*
10. *Post Hoc Ergo Propter Hoc*

1. *Ad hominem* means "against the man" and it is an argument that argues against the person rather than their point of view.

Example: Bernie Sanders is not a good presidential candidate because he's too old.

2. Straw man fallacies mischaracterize an opponent's argument, and then defeat the false arguments.

> *Example*: Candidate Smith: "Plastic bags contribute to environmental pollution and harm to wildlife."
>
> Candidate Jones: "Candidate Smith thinks we can solve all our ecological problems by getting rid of plastic bags."

3. Appeal to ignorance is a misuse of ethos. Appeals to ignorance occur when one believes something to be true that is not, because they do not know enough about the subject, or have not been given enough information to know otherwise.

> *Example*: No one in the Senate objected to the proposed bill, so all Senators must think it's an effective piece of legislation.

4. False dilemmas are also called 'either/or' fallacies. They are arguments that propose there are only two choices, when in fact there may be many more.

> *Example*: Either we cut funding for public television, or we will increase our deficit beyond reasonable bounds.

5. Slippery slope fallacies take a small outcome and spin it out to its worst-case scenario.

> *Example*: If we let the government regulate air quality, before you know it, they'll tell you that you can't smoke in your own house or car.

6. Circular reasoning, also called "begging the question," restates a claim, typically using different words.

Example: Things can't just come from nowhere. Thus, the Big Bang is couldn't have happened.

The premise 'things can't come from nowhere' assumes the Big Bang, being a thing that came from nothing, couldn't have happened. Therefore, the conclusion is assumed in the premise.

7. Overgeneralization often takes the shape of stereotypes or "non-representative samples," that is, taking a small set of examples and assuming that it is true for all.

Example: My aunt smoked four packs of cigarettes a day since age thirteen and lived until age eighty. Therefore, smoking isn't that bad for people.

8. Red Herring fallacies aren't necessarily a failure of logic, but more of a distraction technique.

Example: Mark: It is ethically and legally wrong to cheat on your taxes. Why would you do that?

Karen: Well, what *is* morality exactly?

Mark: It's a code of conduct shared by communities or societies.

Karen: But who created this code? What was their authority to create this code?

9. *Tu Quoque,* also known as an appeal to hypocrisy, intends to discredit an argument by showing that the person making an argument doesn't follow it. It is a combination of *ad hominem* and red herring fallacies.

Example: Fred: You should not be eating cheeseburgers—they are terrible for your health.

Harold: You eat cheeseburgers, too. Obviously, this isn't true.

10. *Post hoc ergo propter hoc* ("after this, therefore because of this") is an informal **fallacy** that states since one event followed another, the first event must have caused the second one. It is often shortened to **post hoc fallacy**.

> *Example*: It rained all day yesterday, and today I have the flue. Rain obviously causes the flu.

There are lots of websites that list other fallacies and give examples. It's less important to know the names and associated examples of all the fallacies than to be able to read your own writing, and the writing of others, and identify places where the writing fails to make its point because it falls into the fallacy trap.

The best way to learn these is to identify them in your reading or viewing. Look at some letters to the editor in a publication—a newspaper or magazine. Try to find examples of any of these fallacies in the letters you read. Summarize the argument, and what fallacy it commits. Think also about how you might rewrite the argument to make it more valid.

Sample 1

What is the main argument?

_____

What fallacy did you find?

_____

_____

How could you argue the point better?

_____

_____

_____

_____

_____

Sample 2

What is the main argument?

_____

What fallacy did you find?

_____

_____

How could you argue the point better?

_____

_____

_____

_____

_____

Sample 3

What is the main argument?

_____

What fallacy did you find?

_____

_____

How could you argue the point better?

_____

_____

_____

_____

_____

Sample 4

What is the main argument?

_____

What fallacy did you find?

_____

_____

How could you argue the point better?

_____

_____

_____

_____

_____

JOURNAL

WRITING TOPICS

INTRODUCTION

This is a space for you to write your answers to some specific topics. Be sure to explain your answers—even if a question doesn't ask *why*, presume the "why" is there.

Be honest with yourself in your answers. You are the only one reading your writing. You will find it more rewarding and instructive if you write your truths, not what you think your truths should be.

Try to write every day—it doesn't have to take long. A 15-minute span of writing can result in some solid ideas and interesting writing. Don't fall into the trap of thinking you need hours in order to accomplish something worthwhile.

There is extra space at the back for any other writing you want to add. What topics have we missed? Write them in.

Write on!

QUESTIONS ABOUT YOU

WRITING TOPICS

1. Describe a quality that you appreciate most in people.

_____

_____

_____

_____

_____

_____

_____

_____

_____

2. Describe what you value most in your leaders.

_____

_____

_____

_____

_____

_____

_____

_____

_____

_____

_____

3. Have you participated in a political rally? What was it about?

_____

_____

_____

_____

_____

_____

_____

_____

_____

_____

4. Who are your heroes right now?

_____

_____

_____

_____

_____

_____

_____

_____

_____

_____

5. Could you be friends with or marry someone with very different views than you have?

_____

_____

_____

_____

_____

_____

_____

_____

_____

6. Who are your heroes in history?

_____

_____

_____

_____

7. What political topic are you undecided about?

8. In what area of your life could you take on a bigger leadership role?

_____

_____

_____

_____

9. If you won ten million dollars in a lottery, but had to give it all away within 24 hours, what would you do with it? (You can't give it to friends or relatives, either.)

_____

_____

_____

_____

_____

_____

_____

_____

_____

_____

10. Do you wear clothing with slogans or sayings on it? What does it say? Why did you choose that?

_____

_____

_____

_____

_____

_____

_____

_____

_____

_____

11. Describe the most difficult political loss or change you've witnessed in your lifetime.

_____

_____

_____

_____

_____

_____

_____

_____

12. If you could ask one person, living or deceased, any question, who and what would you ask? Why?

_____

_____

_____

_____

_____

_____

_____

_____

_____

_____

13. Do you buy organic? Why or why not?

_____

_____

_____

_____

_____

_____

_____

_____

14. Describe any prejudices or biases you're willing to admit to
yourself.

_____

_____

_____

_____

_____

_____

_____

_____

_____

_____

15. Do you consider yourself a pacifist? Why or why not?

_____

_____

_____

_____

_____

_____

_____

_____

_____

16. Imagine you have won the Nobel Prize. What is it for?

_____

_____

_____

_____

_____

_____

_____

_____

_____

17. Do you have "a calling"? What does that mean to you?

_____

_____

_____

_____

_____

_____

_____

_____

18. Would you ever volunteer for medical experimentation? Why or why not?

_____

_____

_____

_____

_____

_____

_____

_____

_____

19. Has an employer or teacher ever treated you unfairly?

_____

_____

_____

_____

_____

_____

_____

_____

_____

20. What risk would you take if you knew you could not fail?

_____

_____

_____

_____

_____

_____

_____

_____

_____

21. What or whom are you a champion for? Why?

_____

_____

_____

_____

_____

_____

_____

_____

_____

22. Describe an issue you try to keep an open mind about.

_____

_____

_____

_____

_____

_____

_____

_____

23. Do you contribute to charity? What do you contribute? What types of charities?

_____

_____

_____

_____

_____

_____

_____

_____

_____

_____

24. Have you contributed to the development of something? What are you most proud of in this development?

_____

_____

_____

_____

_____

_____

_____

_____

_____

25. Describe a time you were passionate about an idea or activity, but then lost interest. What happened?

_____

_____

_____

_____

_____

_____

_____

_____

_____

_____

26. Have you ever sued someone, or wanted to? What was it about?

_____

_____

_____

_____

_____

_____

_____

_____

_____

27. If you started a new business tomorrow, what would it be?

_____

_____

_____

_____

_____

_____

_____

_____

_____

28. How judgmental are you? Describe things or people that you judge regularly.

_____

_____

_____

_____

_____

_____

_____

_____

_____

29. What activities cause you to lose track of time?

_____

_____

_____

_____

_____

_____

_____

_____

_____

30. If you decided to run for public office, what office would it be? What would your campaign slogan be?

_____

_____

_____

_____

_____

_____

_____

_____

_____

31. Describe a time you helped someone through a difficult time.

_____

_____

_____

_____

_____

_____

_____

_____

_____

32. What is the last accomplishment you made that you were really proud of?

_____

_____

_____

_____

_____

_____

_____

_____

_____

33. Would you ever agree to become a spy? If so, for whom, and under what circumstances?

_____

_____

_____

_____

_____

_____

_____

_____

_____

_____

34. If you became a lawyer (or if you are one), what kinds of cases would you not take on? Why?

_____

_____

_____

_____

_____

_____

_____

_____

35. Explain in what ways you are a role model for others in your life.

_____

_____

_____

_____

_____

_____

_____

_____

36. Have you ever done something that you were explicitly forbidden to do?

37. What opportunities have you created for others?

38. Would you ever travel to another country as a missionary? (Or have you?)

_____

_____

_____

_____

_____

_____

_____

_____

_____

39. What three things would you put in a time capsule to be opened in 100 years? What would it say about you, or about your culture?

_____

_____

_____

_____

_____

_____

_____

_____

_____

_____

_____

40. What idea would you want to have crowd-funded on KickStarter or GoFundMe?

_____

_____

_____

_____

_____

_____

_____

_____

_____

41. What are you qualified to teach to others?

_____

_____

_____

_____

_____

_____

_____

_____

_____

_____

_____

42. Describe a time you saved someone's life, or they saved yours.

_____

_____

_____

_____

_____

_____

_____

_____

_____

_____

43. Describe someone who you'd like to trade lives with for a day.

_____

_____

_____

_____

_____

_____

_____

_____

_____

44. Do you consider yourself open-minded or closed-minded in general?

_____

_____

_____

_____

_____

_____

_____

_____

_____

_____

45. Do you consider yourself ambitious? For what?

_____

_____

_____

_____

_____

_____

_____

_____

_____

_____

46. What is the most common topic of discussion over your dinner table (or out with friends, etc.)?

_____

_____
_____
_____
_____
_____
_____
_____
_____

47. Complete this sentence: "Change makes me feel…"

_____
_____
_____
_____
_____
_____
_____
_____
_____

48. If you wrote a will today, who would you leave everything to? (Or, if you have a will, who is your beneficiary?)

_____
_____

49. What topics do you always have an opinion about?

50. What inspires you to be a better person?

---

51. Describe something you hate about politics.

---

52. Describe an event that restored your faith in humanity.

_____

_____

_____

_____

53. Are you a registered voter? Do you vote in every election?

_____

_____

_____

_____

_____

_____

_____

_____

_____

54. What is one thing you could live without?

_____

_____

_____

_____

_____

_____

_____

_____

_____

55. Describe a time someone called you a troublemaker.

_____

_____

_____

_____

_____

_____

_____

_____

56. If you could live in a culture very different from your own, which one would you choose? Describe what appeals to you about that culture.

_____

_____

_____

_____

_____

_____

_____

_____

57. Describe the most interesting person you've ever met.

_____

_____

_____

_____

_____

_____

_____

_____

_____

58. If you dedicated your life to a single cause, what would it be?

_____

_____

_____

_____

_____

_____

_____

_____

_____

_____

_____

59. Describe a time you felt discriminated against, or discriminated against someone else.

_____

_____

_____

_____

_____

_____

_____

_____

60. What profession do you respect most?

_____

_____

_____

_____

_____

_____

_____

_____

_____

61. What historical event do you think had the biggest impact on you or your family?

_____

_____

_____

_____

_____

_____

_____

_____

62. What question do people ask you that you find offensive or annoying?

_____

_____

_____

_____

_____

_____

_____

_____

_____

63. Have you ever, or are you willing to take on bullies?

_____

_____

_____

_____

_____

_____

_____

_____

64. If you could go back in time, would you? To what time period? What would you do once there?

_____

_____

_____

_____

_____

_____

_____

_____

QUESTIONS ABOUT YOUR READING, WRITING, AND VIEWING

1. Which words or phrases do you think you overuse? Why do you overuse them?

_____

_____

_____

_____

_____

_____

_____

_____

_____

2. Do you already keep a journal? How does it help you?

_____

_____

_____

_____

_____

_____

_____

_____

_____

3. Have you ever had anything published?

_____

_____

_____

_____

_____

_____

_____

4. Do you have an effective vocabulary? In what ways do you want to improve it?

_____

_____

_____

_____

_____

_____

_____

_____

_____

_____

5. What inspires your writing ideas most?

_____

_____

_____

_____

_____

_____

_____

_____

_____

6. Write down three phrases or sayings you use nearly every day. Why are they important to you?

_____

_____

_____

_____

_____

_____

_____

_____

_____

7. Do you generally ask a lot of questions or just rely on what you already know?

_____

_____

_____

_____

_____

_____

_____

_____

_____

8. Is there a book you have read multiple times? Which one, and why?

_____

_____

_____

_____

_____

_____

_____

_____

_____

_____

9. What literature or writing course is most memorable to you?

_____

_____

_____

_____

_____

_____

_____

_____

_____

10. What is your favorite documentary film? Why?

_____

_____

_____

_____

_____

_____

_____

_____

_____

_____

11. What children's story do you think sends the wrong message?

_____

_____

_____

_____

_____

_____

_____

_____

12. What is your favorite documentary film? Why?

_____

_____

_____

_____

_____

_____

_____

_____

_____

13. How do you feed your creativity?

_____

_____

_____

_____

_____

_____

_____

_____

_____

14. What have you read recently that has inspired you?

_____

_____

_____

_____

_____

_____

_____

_____

_____

_____

15. Compare your writing style to any author you're familiar with. In what ways are you similar? Different?

_____

_____

_____

_____

_____

_____

_____

_____

_____

16. What book has inspired you the most?

_____

_____

_____

_____

_____

_____

_____

_____

_____

_____

17. Do you have a favorite saying or proverb?

_____

_____

_____

_____

_____

_____

_____

_____

_____

18. If you started a podcast, what would you talk about?

_____

_____

_____

_____

_____

_____

_____

_____

_____

19. If you wrote a children's book, what would it be about?

_____

_____

_____

_____

_____

_____

_____

_____

_____

_____

20. What book or film should be mandatory for everyone?

_____

_____

_____

_____

_____

_____

_____

_____

_____

21. Do you have a favorite reporter or newscaster? What do you like about them?

_____

_____

_____

_____

_____

_____

_____

_____

_____

_____

22. If you were a journalist, what area would you like to cover?

_____

_____

_____

_____

_____

_____

_____

_____

_____

_____

23. Do you think network (not cable or streaming service) shows have too much violence or sexual content?

_____

_____

_____

_____

_____

_____

_____

_____

_____

_____

24. Describe a topic that might come up in conversation that would make you feel completely uninformed.

_____

_____

_____

_____

_____

_____

_____

_____

_____

25. What internet sites do you visit regularly?

_____

_____

_____

_____

_____

_____

_____

_____

_____

_____

26. Are libraries still useful? To whom?

_____

_____

_____

_____

_____

_____

_____

_____

27. What current event are you tired of hearing about in the news?

_____

_____

_____

_____

_____

_____

_____

_____

_____

_____

28. State your position on censorship.

_____

_____

_____

_____

_____

_____

_____

_____

29. Describe your communication style. How does it impact your life?

_____

_____

_____

_____

_____

_____

_____

30. Should there be special laws controlling paparazzi?

31. Which magazines do you read (in paper or online)? Why those?

32. Do you trust what you read online?

_____

_____

_____

_____

_____

_____

_____

_____

_____

QUESTIONS ABOUT YOUR LOCAL ENVIRONMENT

1. Describe your greatest fear about your local culture and government.

_____

_____

_____

_____

_____

_____

_____

_____

_____

2. Describe one major change you feel needs to be made in your city or town.

_____

_____

_____

_____

_____

_____

_____

_____

_____

_____

3. Do you trust your local police?

_____

_____

_____

_____

_____

_____

_____

_____

4. What could you do to make your local civic life better?

_____

_____

_____

_____

_____

_____

_____

_____

_____

_____

5. Name three things about your local area that you find most beautiful.

_____

_____

_____

_____

_____

_____

_____

_____

_____

6. Name three things about your local area you find ugly.

_____

_____

_____

_____

_____

_____

_____

_____

_____

7. What delivery service do you wish you had in your local area?

_____

_____

_____

_____

_____

_____

_____

_____

8. Do you support local businesses in your community? Which ones, and why?

_____

_____

_____

_____

_____

_____

_____

_____

_____

_____

9. Do you give money to homeless people or panhandlers on the street?

_____

_____

_____

_____

_____

_____

_____

_____

_____

_____

10. Describe an industry that is harmful to your local environment.

_____

_____

_____

_____

_____

_____

_____

_____

_____

_____

11. What's one thing you're willing to do today to improve your local area?

_____

_____

_____

_____

_____

_____

_____

_____

_____

12. Imagine you are given ten minutes to talk on a local radio or public access television program. What will you talk about?

_____

_____

_____

_____

_____

_____

_____

_____

_____

13. If you were elected mayor of your city or town, what is the first thing you would do to improve life for everyone?

_____

_____

_____

_____

_____

_____

_____

_____

14. What's the thing you love most about where you live?

_____

_____

_____

_____

_____

_____

_____

_____

_____

15. What local actions should be taken to combat climate change?

_____

_____

_____

_____

_____

_____

_____

_____

_____

QUESTIONS ABOUT THE BIGGER ISSUES

1. Describe your greatest fear about issues with your country's government.

_____

_____

_____

_____

_____

_____

_____

_____

_____

_____

_____

_____

2. Which living public official angers you the most? Explain what makes you angry.

_____

_____

_____

_____

_____

_____

_____

_____

3. What needs to be done on a global scale to combat climate change?

_____

_____

_____

_____

_____

_____

_____

_____

_____

4. Do you think Great Britain should remain in the European Union? (Or, if this change has already happened/not happened, what is your opinion of it?)

_____

_____

_____

_____

_____

_____

_____

_____

_____

5. What is legal that you think should be illegal? Why?

_____

_____

_____

_____

_____

_____

_____

_____

_____

6. What is illegal that you think should be legal? Why?

_____

_____

_____

_____

_____

_____

_____

_____

7. Describe a profession that you think is undervalued. Why is it undervalued? How could this be improved?

_____

_____

_____

_____

_____

_____

_____

_____

_____

_____

_____

8. Describe your feelings about the death penalty.

_____

_____

_____

_____

_____

_____

_____

_____

_____

_____

9. What does "an eye for an eye" mean to you? Do you believe in this concept?

_____

_____

_____

_____

_____

_____

_____

_____

_____

_____

10. In what ways does money impact people negatively?

_____

_____

_____

_____

_____

_____

_____

_____

_____

_____

11. Is plastic pollution a major problem, in your opinion? What should be done?

_____

_____

_____

_____

_____

_____

_____

_____

_____

_____

12. what ways does money impact people positively?

_____

_____

_____

_____

_____

_____

_____

_____

_____

13. What quality do you think all great leaders share?

_____

_____

_____

_____

_____

_____

_____

_____

_____

_____

_____

14. If you could close down one business, what would it be? Why? What would the impact be?

_____

_____

_____

_____

_____

_____

_____

_____

15. What public figure do you disagree with most? What issues do you disagree on in particular?

_____

_____

_____

_____

_____

_____

_____

_____

_____

_____

16. What's a great mystery you would like to solve?

_____

_____

_____

_____

_____

_____

_____

_____

_____

17. Do you believe it is wrong to keep animals in zoos or other places of captivity? Why or why not?

_____

_____

_____

_____

_____

_____

_____

_____

_____

_____

_____

_____

18. Explain your attitudes towards homeschooling.

---

19. If World War III were to happen, what would you do?

---

20. Are there times when one should be confrontational? When? Why?

_____

_____

_____

_____

_____

_____

_____

_____

21. Imagine you meet someone who is over 100 years old. What do you want to ask them?

_____

_____

_____

_____

_____

_____

_____

_____

_____

22. What behavior do you observe in today's society that you think is both common and inappropriate?

_____

_____

_____

_____

_____

_____

_____

_____

_____

23. If you were granted a lunch hour with the top official in your country, what would you want to talk about?

_____

_____

_____

_____

_____

_____

_____

_____

_____

24. What is the biggest enemy to your way of life?

_____

_____

_____

_____

_____

_____

_____

_____

_____

_____

25. Where would you like to explore?

_____

_____

_____

_____

_____

_____

_____

_____

26. How has the internet positively affected our world?

_____

_____

_____

_____

_____

_____

_____

_____

_____

_____

27. How has the internet negatively affected our world?

_____

_____

_____

_____

_____

_____

_____

_____

28. Do you do your absolute best for the environment?

_____

_____

_____

_____

_____

_____

_____

_____

_____

29. Who is the worst world leader alive today?

_____

_____

_____

_____

_____

_____

_____

_____

_____

30. Who is the best world leader alive today?

_____

_____

_____

_____

_____

_____

_____

_____

_____

_____

_____

31. What violations of privacy matter most to you?

_____

_____

_____

_____

_____

_____

_____

_____

_____

32. Describe what war means to the world.

_____

_____

_____

_____

_____

_____

_____

_____

_____

_____

33. What is the most serious issue the planet faces today?

_____

_____

_____

_____

_____

_____

_____

_____

_____

34. Which philanthropist do you admire most today? Why?

_____

_____

_____

_____

_____

_____

_____

_____

_____

35. What are your feelings about or experience with nepotism?

_____

_____

_____

_____

_____

_____

_____

_____

_____

_____

36. Should there be limits on how much money any individual can earn? Why or why not?

_____

_____

_____

_____

_____

_____

_____

_____

_____

_____

37. What famous person has lost your respect or trust? Why?

_____

_____

_____

_____

_____

_____

_____

_____

_____

_____

38. Should tobacco be made illegal?

_____

_____

_____

_____

_____

_____

_____

_____

39. Should heads of charities have salary limits?

_____

_____

_____

_____

_____

_____

_____

_____

_____

_____

_____

40. Is there someone who was not convicted of a crime that should have been, in your opinion?

_____

_____

_____

_____

_____

_____

_____

_____

_____

_____

41. Is there someone who was convicted of a crime that should not have been?

_____

_____

_____

_____

_____

_____

_____

_____

_____

_____

42. What do you think of fracking and oil exploration in sensitive ecosystems?

_____

_____

_____

_____

_____

_____

_____

_____

_____

_____

_____

43. Who has history deemed a "hero" that doesn't deserve this honor?

_____

_____

_____

_____

_____

_____

_____

_____

_____

_____

_____

44. Which animal should be on the endangered species list?

_____

_____

_____

_____

_____

_____

_____

_____

_____

45. What monument do you think needs to be taken down? What should replace it?

_____

_____

_____

_____

_____

_____

_____

_____

_____

46. State your position on GMOs in food.

_____

_____

_____

_____

_____

_____

_____

_____

47. State your opinion on space travel and exploration.

_____

_____

_____

_____

_____

_____

_____

_____

_____

_____

48. Should prisoners be forced to work?

_____

_____

_____

_____

_____

_____

_____

_____

49. What do you think would be a good first step in eliminating poverty?

_____

_____

_____

_____

_____

_____

_____

_____

_____

_____

50. What national holiday should be added to the calendar? Which one should be eliminated?

_____

_____

_____

_____

_____

_____

_____

_____

51. What role should public transportation have in modern life?

_____

_____

_____

_____

_____

_____

_____

_____

_____

_____

52. Should whaling be legal?

_____

_____

_____

_____

_____

_____

_____

_____

_____

53. It is sometimes said that "justice is blind." Do you think this is true?

_____

_____

_____

_____

_____

OTHER IDEAS

WRITING SPACE FOR OTHER IDEAS YOU HAVE

_____

_____

_____

_____

_____

_____

_____

_____

_____

_____

_____

_____

_____

YOUR WRITING PROJECTS

Plan your next three writing projects. For each project, describe your goal, that is, what you want your audience to do or feel as a result of reading your work, the type of writing you'll do, and who your audience is.

Project 1

Title:

_____

Goal:

_____

_____

Type of document:

_____

Audience:

_____

Notes:

_____

_____

_____

_____

_____

Project 2

Title:

_____

Goal:

_____

_____

Type of document:

_____

Audience:

_____

Notes:

_____

_____

_____

_____

_____

Project 3

Title:

_____

Goal:

_____

_____

Type of document:

_____

Audience:

_____

Notes:

_____

_____

_____

_____

_____

AFTERWORD

This workbook/journal accompanies the edx.org course that I teach called "Writing for Social Justice." However, you do not need to take the course to make use of this book. All the material here is independent from the course, and primarily prompts you to write about what matters to you and find the issues that you want to influence.

Made in the USA
Monee, IL
10 September 2022

13641516R00075